Look What Came From

Greece

by

Kevin Davis

Franklin Watts

A Division of Grolier Publishing

New York London Hong Kong Sydney

Danbury, Connecticut

Series Concept: Shari Joffe
Design: Steve Marton

Library of Congress Cataloging-in-Publication Data

Davis, Kevin A.
   Look What Came From Greece / by Kevin Davis.
      p. cm. — (Look what came from)
   Includes bibliographical references and index.
   Summary: Describes many things that originally came
from Greece, including inventions, entertainment, sports,
government, medicine, architecture, food, and words.
   ISBN 0-531-11744-8 (lib. bdg.)   0-531-15974-4(pbk.)
   1. Civilization—Greek influences Juvenile literature.
2. Greece—Civilization Juvenile literature. [1. Greece—
Civilization. 2. Civilization—Greek influences.]
I. Title. II. Series: Look what came from series.
DF741.D36 1999
938—dc21   99-19257
                                                      CIP
                                                       AC

Visit Franklin Watts on the Internet at:
http://publishing.grolier.com

Photo credits ©: Archive Photos: 7 top right; Art Resource, NY: 10; Bridgeman Art
Library International Ltd., London/New York: 13 left (STC96501 Eriphile, costume
for "Iphigenia in Aulis" by Jean Racine, from Volume II of "Research of the
Costumes and Theatre of All Nations", engraved by Pierre Michel Alix, 1802,
coloured engraving by Philippe Cherry/Private Collection, The Stapleton
Collection), 15 (BAL99068 Black figured Panathenaic amphora, detail of a boxing
contest, Greek c. 336 BC/British Museum, London, UK.), 12 right (AMQ104779
Two Statuettes of elderly comic actors, Greek, from at Attica, c. 375-350 BC, clay
with white slip/Ashmolean Museum, Oxford, UK); Charise Mericle: 5; Corbis-
Bettmann: border on pages 4, 6-32 (Mimmo Jodice), cover left, 22 left (Craig
Lovell), 8 left (UPI), cover bottom right, 7 bottom right, 7 bottom left, 9 right, 11
left, 16, 17 left; Gamma-Liaison, Inc.: 22 center (Michael Gallagher), 4 (Sheila
Nardulli); North Wind Picture Archives: 6 right, 8 right, 9 left, 12 left, 18, 19;
Omni-Photo Communications: 24 left (Grace Davies); Photo Researchers: 3, 21
right (Carlyn Iverson), 25 top right (Mehau Kulyk/SPL), 17 right (Andy Levin), 24
right (Renee Lynn), 25 top left (Doug Martin); Stock Boston: 14 (Bob Daemmrich);
Stock Montage, Inc.: 6 left, 20; Superstock, Inc.: 13 right (Museo Archeologico
Naples, Italy/A.K.G, Berlin), cover top right, 12 center (The Lowe Art Museum,
The University of Miami), 11 right, 21 left, 25 bottom right, 25 bottom left; Tom
Pantages: back cover, 23 top right, 23 bottom right, 32; Tony Stone Images: 1, 22
right, 23 left, 27 (Chris Everard), cover background (John Lamb), 7 top left
(Dennis O'Clair).

Contents

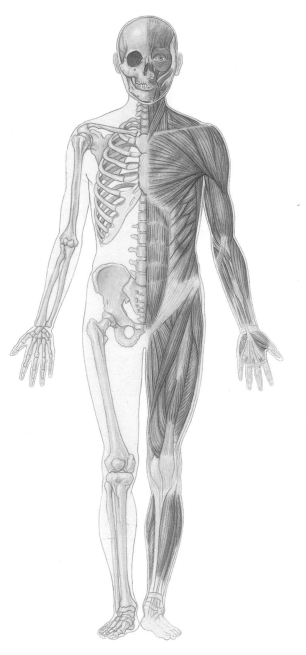

Greetings from Greece!

Greece is a beautiful country with a fascinating history. It is located in southern Europe, across the Mediterranean Sea from Africa. Greece also has thousands of little islands.

The flag of Greece

Thousands of years ago, Greece had one of the most advanced civilizations in the world. This civilization, known as ancient Greece, lasted from about 3000 B.C. to about 300 B.C. Ancient Greece was a center for education, art, science, and philosophy. Many important traditions, inventions, and ideas that are still used today came from ancient Greece.

The Olympics, theaters, libraries, and delicious foods like spinach pie are just a few of Greece's contributions to the world. So let's take a trip to Greece to find out what comes from this great place!

Education

Greek people have always believed that education is very important. The Greeks were the first to open organized **schools,** in the city of Athens, more than 2,000 years ago. The Greeks believed that citizens should have a good education. The first schools were for males only. Later, schools were open to everyone.

An artist's impression of the first public library

Ancient Greek painting showing scenes from the School of Athens

Many people believe that the first public **library** was built in Greece. The first libraries didn't have books as we know them. Back then, people wrote on a type of paper called papyrus that was rolled up into scrolls.

Most libraries today have a set of books called an **encyclopedia.** Encyclopedias also

Archimedes

Euclid

Pythagoras

came from Greece. They contain information about lots of different subjects. In ancient Greece, the first encyclopedias were written to help students get a well-rounded education. Today, many encyclopedias can be read on computers!

In school, you probably have learned some **math.** Did you know that many important kinds of math, like **fractions** and **geometry,** were developed by Greeks? Pythagoras, Euclid, and Archimedes were Greek scholars who worked out some of the basic rules of math that are still used today.

Inventions

Clothes irons from the 1400s (front) and 1800s (back)

The Greeks invented the first **clothes iron** about 2,400 years ago. They used a heated metal bar shaped like a rolling pin to smooth out wrinkles in their clothes. They also used this iron to create pleats, which are creases in clothing. Today's irons have flat bottoms and are heated by electricity.

Have you ever looked at a **map?** For many thousands of years, people who owned land had maps of their own property. The Greeks were the first people to draw maps of very large areas for travelers. They also made the first maps of the stars.

Ancient Greek map of the world

Ancient catapult

Before guns and cannons were invented, wars were fought with bows and arrows, swords, and rocks. The Greeks invented a weapon called a **catapult.** This device had a long arm that was pulled back and released to throw rocks long distances at enemies during battles. It could hurl rocks as far as 1,000 feet (305 m)!

Architecture

Ruins of an ancient Greek building

The Greeks were very good builders. They made beautiful homes and temples from stone and marble. Many of these buildings were surrounded by **columns,** which are tall, round pillars. The Greeks created three important types of column designs which are still used today. A **Doric** column is plain. An **Ionic** column has scrolls on it. **Corinthian** columns have carvings in the shapes of leaves.

Doric column

Ionic column

Corinthian column

Many thousands of years ago, people had a hard time crossing over rivers. They would have to wait for a tree to fall over a river to get across. The Greeks are believed to have built the first **bridge,** out of logs that were tied together. Later, they learned to make bridges from stone.

Ancient bridge in Greece

11

Entertainment

Artist's impression of an ancient Greek theater

Going to the theater was a regular part of Greek life. Actors are people who perform in plays. In ancient Greece, men played both the women's and men's parts. Actors usually put on costumes and wore masks that had a happy face or a sad face. They performed in **tragedies,** which were sad stories, or **comedies,** which were funny.

Have you ever seen a play? Maybe you've been in one at school. The Greeks were the first people to put on plays at **theaters.** Many theaters were built on hillsides so the audience could hear and see the actors on stage.

Ancient Greek theater mask

A nineteenth-century production of an Ancient Greek tragedy

Ancient Greek painting showing a scene from Greek theater

The Greeks also were the first to use **special effects** in the theater. If they wanted to make the sound of a rainstorm, they rolled lots of little rocks over a sheet of metal. In some Greek plays, a person would be lifted up by a rope to make it look as if he were flying!

Sports

One of the most popular sporting events in the world came from Greece more than 2,000 years ago. The **Olympics,** which today are held every four years, began as small athletic contests at Greek religious festivals. The contests were for men and boys only. It was not until modern times that women were allowed to compete in the Olympics.

Early Olympic contests included running races and events such as discus throwing, the long jump, wrestling, horse racing, and the javelin throw. **Boxing,** which was invented in Greece, was also a common sport in the early games.

The Olympic Games begin with the lighting of the Olympic torch.

Ancient Greek painting of boxers

15

more sports

Ancient Greek stadium during the Olympic Games

The Greeks were also the first people to build large **stadiums** where people went to watch these athletic contests. One of the biggest stadiums was built in the city of Olympia, between two hills. As many as 40,000 spectators could watch the games at this incredible stadium.

Pheidippides announcing the victory at Marathon to the people of Athens

A very long running race called the **marathon** also came from ancient Greece. It was named after a city called Marathon, where the Greeks fought the Persians in a war. When the Greeks won, they sent a messenger named Pheidippides from Marathon to Athens to tell the Greek people about their victory. He ran the entire distance of about 25 miles (40 km) without stopping and died after arriving. Today, marathon races are 26.2 miles (42 km) and are held all over the world.

Modern-day marathon

Government

Long ago, many countries were ruled by kings or emperors. People did not choose their leaders. The Greeks were the first to come up with the idea of **democracy.** This means "rule by the people." In a democracy, people are involved in running their government and choosing their leaders. The first democracy was started in Athens. At that time, only male citizens were allowed to take part.

With democracy came the practice of allowing people to **vote.** Greeks held events called **assemblies.** These were public meetings in which citizens were allowed to talk about important issues where they lived. They had debates and everyone was allowed to speak.

Assembly meeting in ancient Greece

Today, most countries have independent cities or states. This idea also came from ancient Greece. The Greeks created city-states, which were areas of land that had their own governments and leaders. The ancient Greek models for democracy and city-states are used in countries all over the world today.

Map of the southern part of ancient Greece

Medicine

In ancient times, people did not know much about treating illnesses. People often prayed in hopes of getting better. A Greek doctor named Hippocrates came up with a new method for treating sick people. He developed the practice of diagnosis, which means that he examined people and wrote down their symptoms. Then he came up with ways to try to make them better with medicine or a special diet. Hippocrates is known as the Father of Medicine.

Hippocrates also created a set of special rules for doctors known as the Hippocratic Oath. The oath is a doctor's promise to be

Hippocrates

honest with patients, to protect and preserve life, and to keep information about patients private.

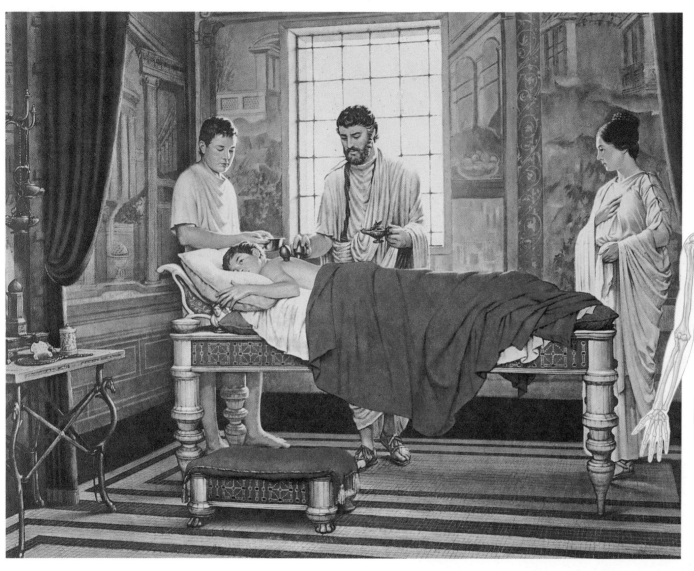

Ancient Greek doctor treating a patient

Another Greek scientist, Herophilus, was one of the first people to study **anatomy**— the parts of the body and how they work.

He named different parts of the body and put drawings of them into a book.

Modern-day drawing of human anatomy

Food

Feta cheese

Some delicious foods that are enjoyed around the world originally came from Greece. Greek restaurants are popular in cities everywhere. You can probably find some of these foods at restaurants where you live.

Many Greek foods, such as **dolmades,** are served in small, snack-sized portions.

Dolmades

This famous, ancient food is made with fresh vine leaves stuffed with meat, rice, and herbs.

Tzatziki is a creamy dip made with cucumbers, Greek yogurt, and herbs. Greeks like to dip their snacks in tzatziki or spread it on certain foods.

Feta cheese is the most popular of Greek cheeses. It is used in many dishes and in Greek salads. Feta is a soft, white, salty cheese. It is made from goat milk, sheep's milk, or cow's milk.

Greeks are very fond of grilling meats such as lamb and pork. **Souvlaki** is marinated meat that is put on skewers and cooked over an open fire or barbecue. Sometimes vegetables are put on the skewer, too. People also call this shishkebob or kebabs. Another popular Greek dish, **spanakopita,** is a spinach-and-herb pie made with a flaky, buttery dough called phyllo.

For dessert, Greeks love to eat a rich and sweet pastry called **baklava,** which is also made with phyllo. Between many thin layers of dough are ground walnuts, almonds, and a gooey honey sauce. It's delicious!

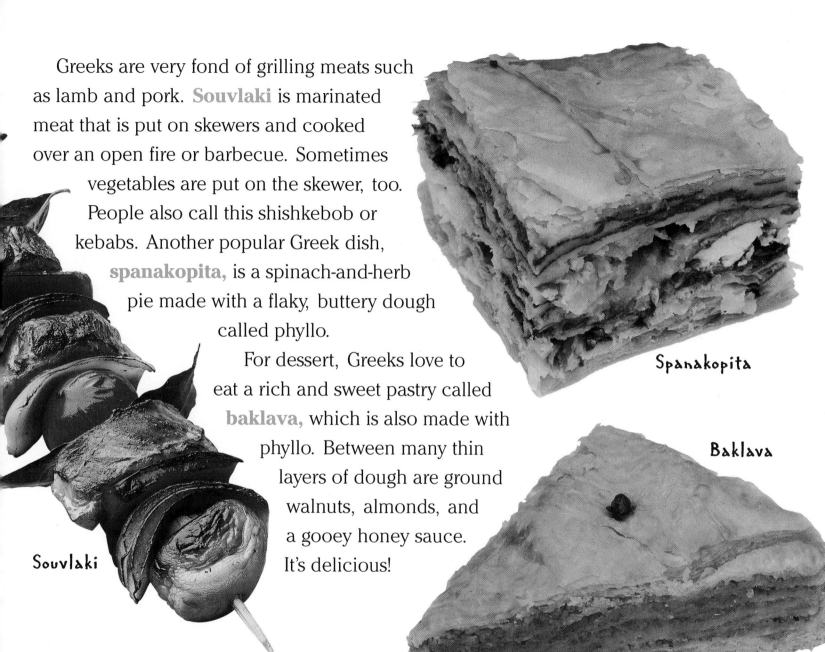

Spanakopita

Baklava

Souvlaki

Words

Bicycle

Many words that we use today came from the Greek language. Here are some words you might know:

"**Alphabet**" comes from the words *alpha* and *beta*, which are the first two letters of the Greek alphabet.

ΑΒΧΔΕΦΓΗΙϑΚΛΜΝΟΠΘΡΣΤΥςΩΞΨΖ

The Greek alphabet

"**Bicycle**" comes from the word *bi*, which means "two," and *kyklos*, which means "wheel."

"**Gymnasium**" comes from the word *gymnasia*, which originally was a place in Greece for sports and learning.

"**Hippopotamus**" comes from *hippos*, which means "horse," and *potamos*, which means "river." The hippopotamus looks like a giant horse that lives in the water!

24

Gymnasium

Planets

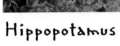
Hippopotamus

Rhinoceros

"Planet" comes from *planetes*, which means "wandering." The Greek words *planetes asteres* mean "wandering stars."

"Rhinoceros" is from the Greek words *rhino*, which means "nose," and *keros*, which means "horn." A rhinoceros has a big horn on its head.

A Recipe from Greece

Here is an easy and tasty recipe for a traditional Greek food that you can make in just a few minutes!

Tzatziki

To start, you'll need the following ingredients:

- 1 medium cucumber, peeled
- 1 clove of garlic, crushed, or 1 teaspoon of garlic powder
- 3 scallions (green onions)
- 1 teaspoon of olive oil
- 1/2 teaspoon of white vinegar
- 1 teaspoon of fresh dill, finely chopped
- 1 cup of plain yogurt

You'll also need the following equipment:

- a cutting knife (to be used with adult supervision)
- a carrot peeler (to be used with adult supervision)
- a garlic press
- a cutting board
- a small bowl

Directions:

1. Use a carrot peeler to peel the skin off the cucumber.

2. Cut the cucumber in half lengthwise and scoop out the seeds. Cut the cucumber into very small pieces, and put them in a small bowl.

3. Peel the papery skin off the garlic clove and then crush the garlic in the garlic press. Add this to the bowl.

4. Chop the scallions finely and add them to the bowl.

5. Chop the dill finely and add it to the bowl.

6. Add the olive oil and vinegar.

7. Add the yogurt and stir gently. Cover and chill for two hours or more.

Dip your favorite vegetables or crackers in the tzatziki!

Tzatziki served with souvlaki

How do you say...?

People in Greece speek Greek. Greek uses a different alphabet than English does. Try saying some words in Greek yourself!

English	Greek	How to pronounce it
hello	Γεια σας	ya sas
goodbye	Αντίο	ahn-DEE-o
actor	ηθοποιός	ith-o-pee-OHS
bridge	γέφυρα	YEH-fir-a
building	χτίριο	h-TI-rio
cheese	τυρί	ti-RI
clothes iron	σίδηρο	SID-hiro
government	κυβέρνηση	ky-VER-ni-si
map	χάρτης	HAR-tis
sport	άθλημα	ATH-li-ma

To find out more

Here are some other resources to help you learn more about Greece:

Books

Chrisp, Peter, and Hayden, Kate. **Ancient Greece** (My World series). World Book Inc., 1999.

Kerr, Daisy. **Ancient Greeks** (Worldwise series). Franklin Watts, 1997.

Nardo, Don. **Ancient Greece** (World History series). Lucent Books, 1994.

Pearson, Anne. **Ancient Greece** (Eyewitness Books). Knopf, 1992.

Stein, R. Conrad. **Athens** (Cities of the World series). Children's Press, 1997.

Organizations and Online Sites

Ancient Greek Artifacts
http://www.rmplc.co.uk/eduweb/ sites/allsouls/bm/ag1.html
A photographic tour of ancient Greek artifacts from the British Museum.

Civilizations: Greece and Rome
http://www.richmond.edu/~ed344/ 98/greecerome/civ.html
A site that takes you on a journey through these two fascinating ancient civilizations. Includes information on geography, government, agriculture, architecture, the arts, religion, sports, and the roles of men, women, and children in ancient Greece.

Go Greece
http://www.gogreece.com/
A great site on Greece that includes maps, a cookbook, a cultural tour, news, entertainment, sports, government resources, a search engine, and much more.

Greece
http://expedia.msn.com/wg/places/ greece/HSFS/htm
A great site with fast facts, history, mythology, almanac, food, culture, and many links.

Map of Ancient Greece
http://www.princeton.edu/ ~markwoon/Myth/myth-maps.html
Interesting site that compares a map of how ancient Greece really looked with a map of how the ancient Greeks thought it looked.

Glossary

ancient very old

architecture buildings

citizen person who is born in or is made a member of a city, country, or nation

civilization the way of life of a people

contribution the act of giving something

discus a heavy disk used in athletic contests to see who can throw it the greatest distance

independent belonging to no one, free from influence or control

javelin a long, spearlike pole used for throwing in a sporting contest

marinated when meats or vegetables are soaked in sauce to give them flavor

model a thing that is worth imitating

oath a promise to do something or act a certain way

papyrus a tall grasslike plant used by ancient people to make paper

philosophy a certain way of thinking; a search for wisdom or knowledge to explain things

rotisserie a device for roasting meat by rotating it slowly over a fire

scholars people who are experts on certain subjects

scrolls rolled-up pieces of paper with writing on them

spectators people who gather to watch events such as sports or plays

traditions customs or ways of life handed down from generation to generation

Index

Look what doesn't come from Greece!

Gyros are delicious sandwiches made with slices of ground lamb stuffed in pita bread with tzatziki sauce and onions. Gyros are very popular at Greek restaurants. But it is believed they were invented in New York, where they were sold at lunch counters and by street vendors. The word "gyros" comes from the Greek word *gyros*, which means "to turn." The lamb used in gyros is cooked on a device called a rotisserie, which turns the meat as it cooks.

Meet the Author

Kevin Davis loves to travel and write about interesting places. He is an author and journalist who lives in Chicago. This book is dedicated to his sister, Laura Davis.